Santa's North Pole Friends
ACTIVITY BOOK

S0-DHV-401

Snowflake Pairs

Color matching snowflakes with the same color.

Decorate These Yummy Cookies!

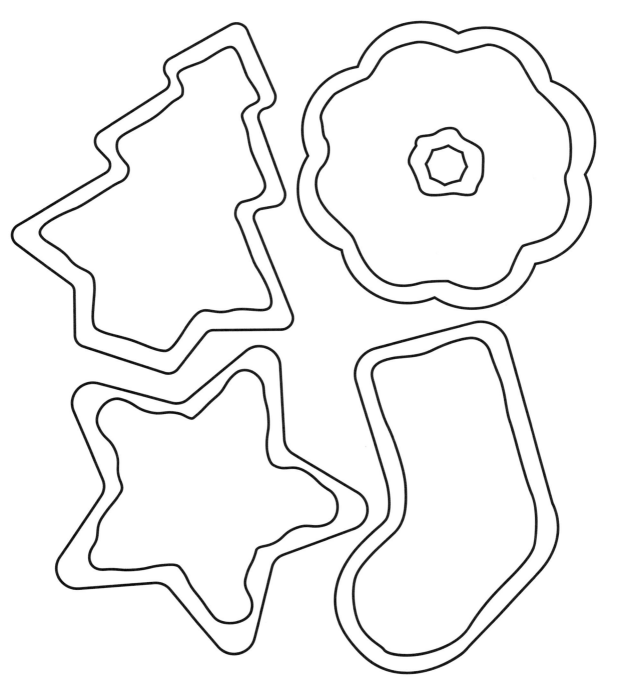

Christmas Tree Maze

Can you find your way to the top star?

START

See answer key at end of book.

How Many Lights Can You Count?

Answer: 15

'Twas the Night Before Christmas

Color the room and decorate with stickers.

Winter Wonder Word Search

Look up, down, across and diagonally to find these words.

MAGIC
SNOW
MERRY
BELIEVE
JOLLY
BRIGHT

```
B M S N O W
E B E M L J
L N T R U G
I J H M R U
E O G A T Y
V L I G N K
E L R I D E
C Y B C K Y
```

See answer key at end of book.

Letter Maze

Color the connecting squares that spell out
HOHOHO MERRY CHRISTMAS

C	H	H	M	R	A	R	C	H	Y
H	O	I	O	M	E	R	H	O	R
T	H	O	H	R	R	R	M	H	S
R	O	M	A	C	O	Y	I	C	T
H	O	Y	M	H	Y	C	H	R	I
Y	M	H	R	H	O	O	R	I	O
H	I	T	S	M	H	H	I	T	S
R	H	O	I	C	T	T	S	T	Y
M	H	H	I	T	S	M	A	M	Y
R	A	R	C	H	Y	A	C	A	T
I	C	T	R	H	O	S	O	S	A

See answer key at end of book.

Fill in the Snow Globe

Draw and color something special for Christmas.

Pile Up the Presents

Color each path to help the
Scout Elf fill Santa's sleigh.

orange
red
green
blue

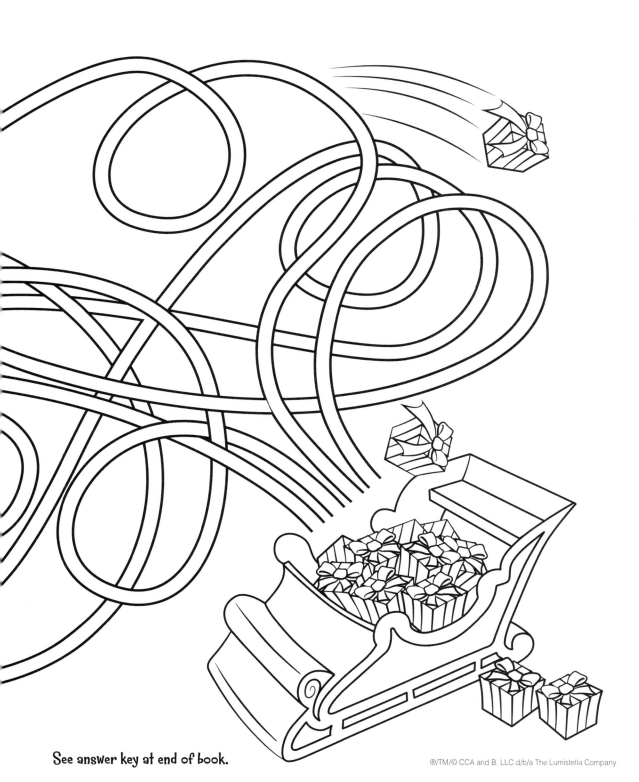

See answer key at end of book.

Sweet Snack Stack

How many of each snack are in the wheelbarrow?

Fill in the number for each snack.

Answers:
3 cookies
5 candies
4 cups of cocoa
4 donuts

Collect Treats for the Elf Pets®

Help the Elf Pets® Reindeer find his way to the barn by connecting all the carrots.

Help the Elf Pets® St. Bernard pup find his way to the doghouse by connecting all the treats.

Help the Elf Pets® Arctic Fox cub find her way to her den by connecting all the blueberries.

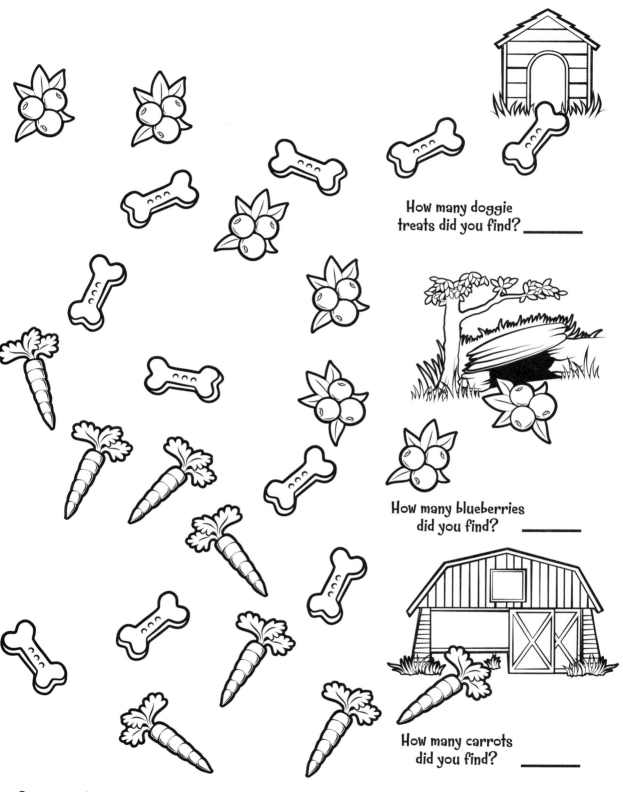

How many doggie
treats did you find? _____

How many blueberries
did you find? _____

How many carrots
did you find? _____

See answer key at end of book.

On the 12th Day of Christmas,

Match the sticker to the gift beside each number.

Place ONE sticker here

12 Christmas cookies...

Place ONE sticker here

11 Shiny trinkets...

10 Jingling sleigh bells...

Place ONE sticker here

9 Silly snowmen...

Place ONE sticker here

8 Soaring reindeer...

Place ONE sticker here

Place ONE sticker here

7 Cups of cocoa...

My Scout Elf Gave To Me...

Place ONE sticker here

6 Trilling trumpets...

Place ONE sticker here

5 Candy canes...

Place ONE sticker here

4 Piled-up presents...

3 Snow globes...

Place ONE sticker here

Place ONE sticker here

2 Christmas trees...

Place ONE sticker here

...And a card written "See you next year!"

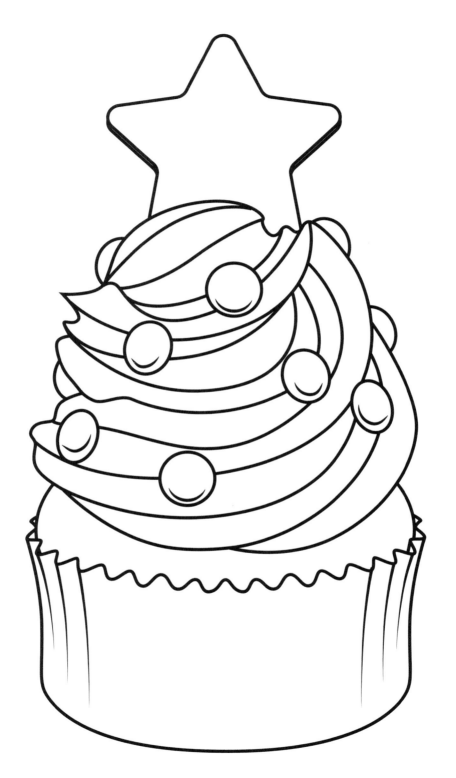

Sweet Dreams!

Draw and color this Saint Bernard's dream.

Connect the Dots

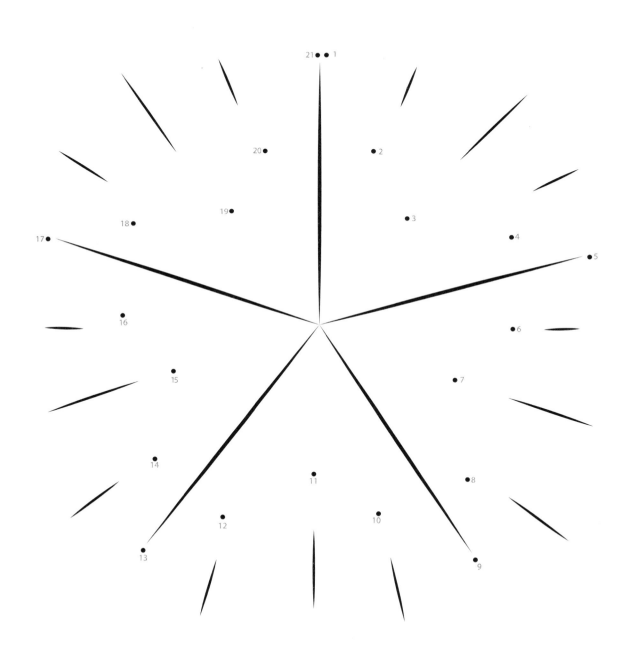

Global Explorer

Fun Fact:

Scout Elves know
over 6,000 languages.

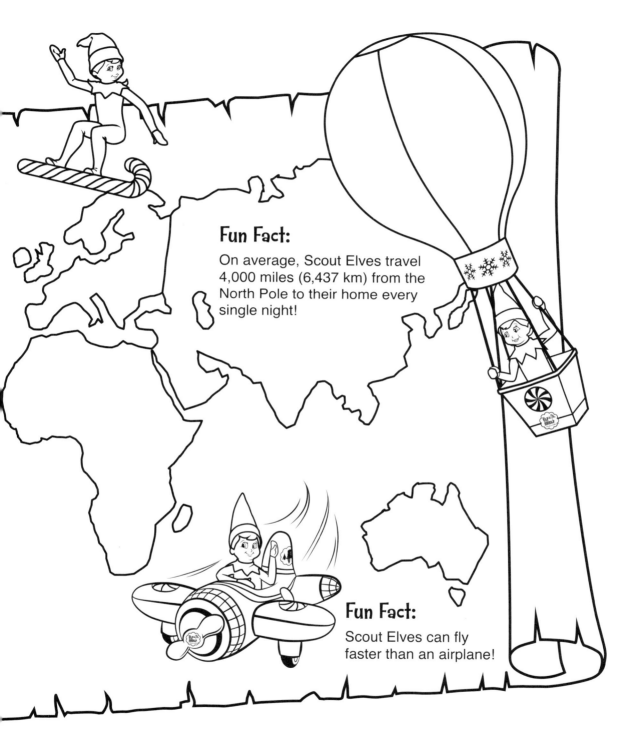

Fun Fact:

On average, Scout Elves travel 4,000 miles (6,437 km) from the North Pole to their home every single night!

Fun Fact:

Scout Elves can fly faster than an airplane!

Color the map.

It's a Scout Elf Party!

How many Scout Elves do you see?

Answer: 10

Find the Pikku Deer

Find and color all the Elf Pets® Reindeer.

Find out more about the legendary pikku deer in the animated special
Elf Pets: Santa's Reindeer Rescue.

How many Elf Pets®
Reindeer did you find?

Color
My Outfit!

Color
My Outfit!

Scout Elf Secret Code

Use the key to decode three
special messages from the Scout Elves.

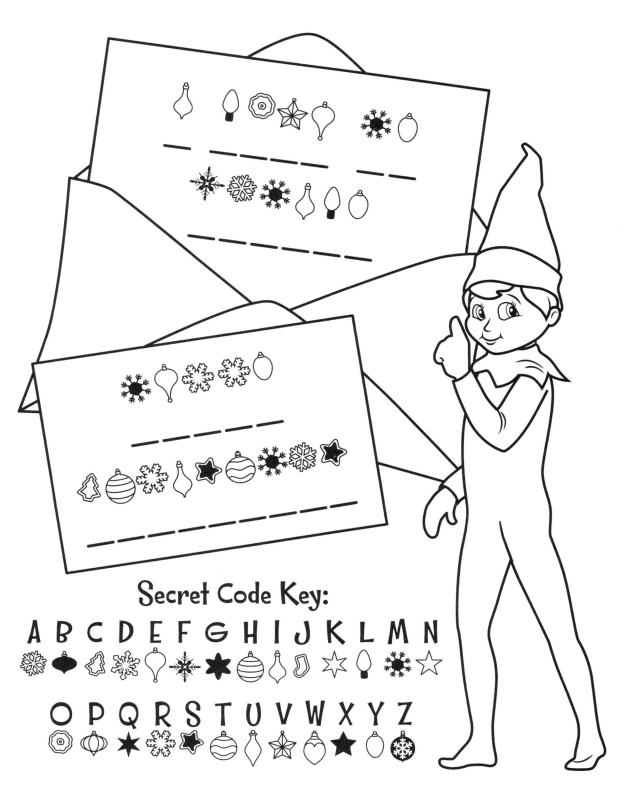

Secret Code Key:

A B C D E F G H I J K L M N

O P Q R S T U V W X Y Z

Wacky Sled Race

Which path will lead you to the finish line?

START

1   2   3

FINISH!

See answer key at end of book.

Finish Drawing the Scout Elf's Face

Skirt Sketch

Add designs and colors to these blank skirts.

So Charming!

Match the correct charm to Santa's Elf Pets®.

Color the Elf Pets®
and find the right
heart charm for each
one on the next page.

A

Color each charm, then fill in the letter for the correct charm of the Elf Pets® on the opposite page.

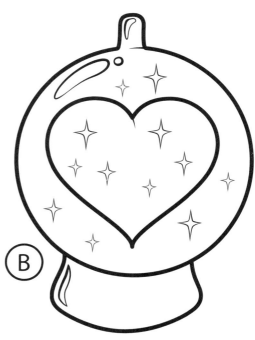

B

C

®/TM/© CCA and B, LLC d/b/a The Lumistella Company

Shadow Play

Circle the Scout Elf's true shadow.

3.

2.

1.

4.

Answer: 4

My Scout Elf's Name Is:

....

My Scout Elf's Favorite Hiding Spots Are:

....

....

....

....

....

....

....

It's Cocoa Time!

Guide the Scout Elf to the cup of hot cocoa.

Start Here

See answer key at end of book.

®/TM/© CCA and B, LLC d/b/a The Lumistella Company

Who's on Santa's Sleigh?

Connect the dots, then color.

R=Red   B=Brown
Y=Yellow O=Orange
L=Light Blue

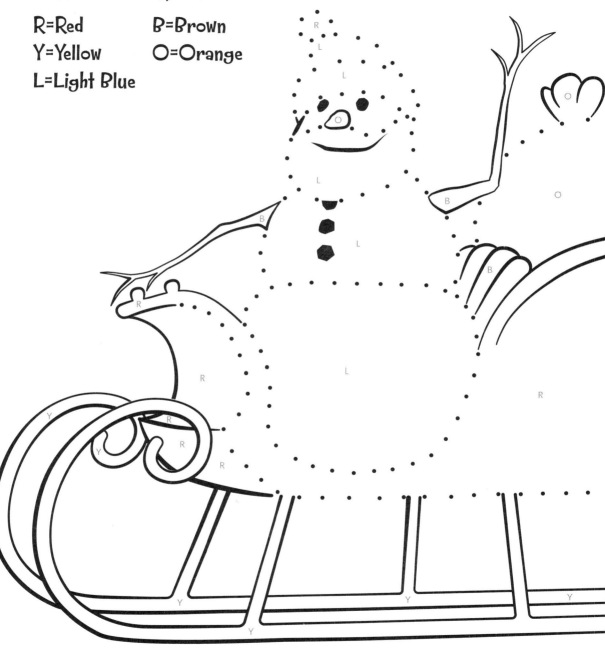

Snow Day Maze

Help the Scout Elf find his snowman pal.

Start

See answer key at end of book.

Decorate the House
for the Holidays

Connect the Dots to Finish the Scout Elf

Connect the Dots and Color

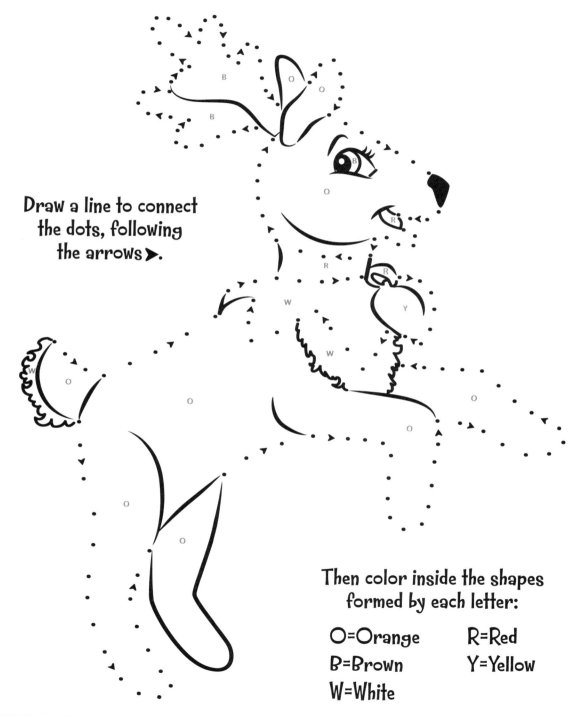

Draw a line to connect the dots, following the arrows ➤.

Then color inside the shapes formed by each letter:

O=Orange   R=Red

B=Brown   Y=Yellow

W=White

Sort the Wreaths

Help the elves find which wreath belongs to them.

See answer key at end of book.

How Many Snowflakes Can You Count?

Barn Dash

Follow the carrots to find your way!

Start

Finish

See answer key at end of book.

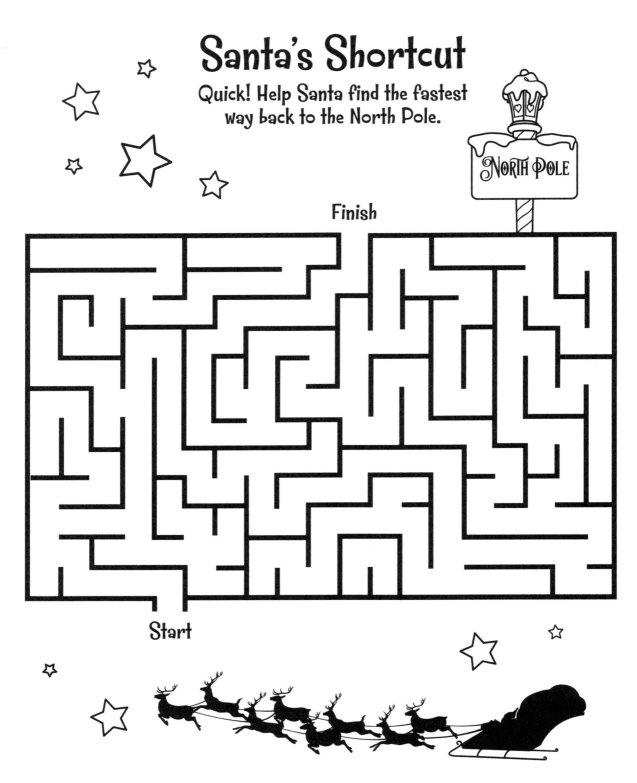

Santa's Shortcut

Quick! Help Santa find the fastest way back to the North Pole.

NORTH POLE

Finish

Start

See answer key at end of book.

Color by Letter

A=Red   B=Orange   C=Yellow   D=Brown   E=Blue   F=Green   G=Violet
No Letter=White

®/TM/© CCA and B, LLC d/b/a The Lumistella Company

Draw Your Own Scout Elf!

Starting at the top of this picture, count across each row of squares
until you see a line or a shape in a square. . .

. . . then draw that line or shape in the same square in the grid below. Do the same for all squares until you complete the picture.

	1	2	3	4	5	6	7	8	9
A									
B									
C									
D									
E									
F									
G									
H									
I									
J									

Decorate the Tree

Color by Numbers

1=Green 2=Yellow 3=Blue 4=Red 5=Brown 6=Orange

Christmas Spirit Word Search

E	L	F	Z	H	F	E	Q	M	U	X	E
Z	H	A	E	Q	M	U	X	E	L	R	S
C	R	S	I	J	G	E	Y	K	O	L	W
O	G	K	M	N	E	R	B	W	V	R	T
F	A	I	T	H	Z	H	F	U	E	Q	R
Y	C	H	E	L	R	J	S	A	F	X	E
L	A	V	G	I	H	D	R	L	A	M	I
F	N	E	S	X	N	O	L	F	V	E	N
S	E	R	U	P	A	E	P	Y	G	R	D
Z	H	F	E	Q	M	U	X	E	L	T	E
A	J	W	S	E	T	N	A	D	R	C	E
R	S	A	N	T	A	L	S	R	J	O	R

Color the squares that spell out:

FAITH   HOPE   LOVE

Can you find the three secret words?

SCOUT _ _ _

_ _ _ _ _ _ CLAUS

ELF PETS® _ _ _ _ _ _ _ _ _

See answer key at end of book.

Good Deed List

Write down all the nice things you've done.

....

....

....

....

....

....

....

....

....

....

....

Color the Cookies for Santa

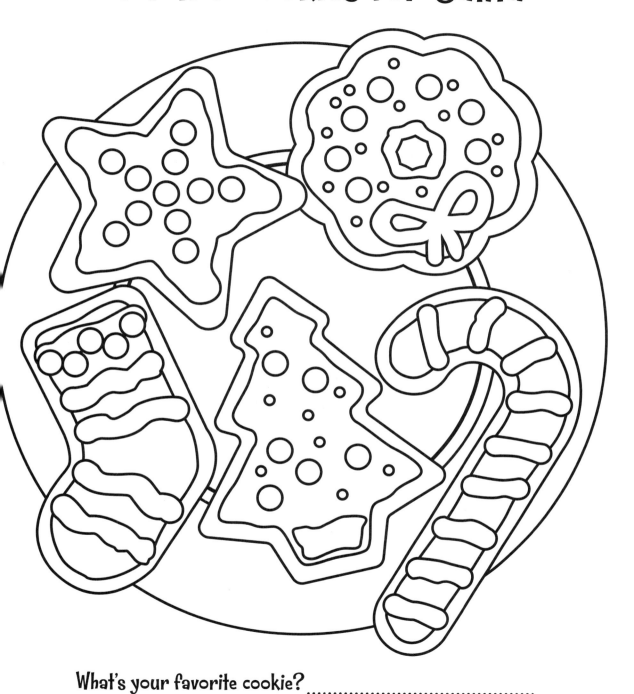

What's your favorite cookie? ....

Christmas Cookies!

Christmas Star Maze

Can you find your way to the center of the Christmas Star?

Start

Draw This Reindeer's Happiest Daydream

Reindeer Name Generator

This reindeer needs a name. Use the initials from your first and last names to create something fun!

Find the first letter of your first name ...

A - Mistletoe	G - Wiggles	M - Lightning	S - Cocoa	Y - Sugar
B - Chestnut	H - Cinnamon	N - Captain	T - Speedy	Z - Spark
C - Sprinkles	I - Hickory	O - Flash	U - Blizzard	
D - Admiral	J - Bootsie	P - Peppermint	V - Pecan	
E - Patches	K - Dizzy	Q - Gumdrop	W - Jolly	
F - Zip	L - Snuggles	R - Dazzles	X - Apples	

Find the first letter of your last name ...

A - Whiskerson	G - Bellingham	M - Charmerson	S - Flufferstein	Y - Berryman
B - von Stride	H - Wonderland	N - Frostino	T - McMittens	Z - Delightwell
C - Rocketberg	I - Gallopsalot	O - Snoweridge	U - Flutterley	
D - McJingles	J - Hooveski	P - O'Flurry	V - Sleighski	
E - Darlington	K - Wishesbee	Q - Tinseltoes	W - Snugglewell	
F - von Whimsy	L - Slushbucket	R - Hoovington	X - Winterton	

Your new reindeer name is:

....

North Pole Mail Call!

Put stickers, addresses and labels on the mail.

String the Lights

Connect all the holiday lights by drawing only one line.

See answer key at end of book.

This Scout Elf is Hungry!

Help him find his way
to a tasty snack.

Start

Ho-Ho-Ho Holiday Scramble

Help the Scout Elf unscramble the letters and
write out each word.

SSOIGNKTC ....

RWAEHT ....

SMSRCHITA ....

ATSR ....

KOCIOES ....

ITSGF ....

OTSY ....

RYERM ....

Hidden Holiday Words

The Scout Elves have hidden eight words in this word search.
Look up, down, across and diagonally to find them.

CHRISTMAS   WREATH
PRESENTS   ELVES
TREE   SANTA
COOKIES   CANDY CANES

```
C V J S Q M M Q O C T H
A E C E E W W R E A T H
N L R M U A H P L V W H
D I M E S A E B V S C T
Y T P L W O R Q E Y O W
C H R I S T M A S V O O
A L E Z I P T M M Z K E
N N S T U A A K R I I M
E A E Q R S S B U A E S
S S N E A E I U S P S C
J O T T E O E G C U A Q
C C S L P S A N T A E S
```

Decorate the Wreath

Answer Keys

Christmas Tree Maze

Can you find your way to the top star?

START

Winter Wonder Word Search

Look up, down, across and diagonally to find these words.

MAGIC
SNOW
MERRY
BELIEVE
JOLLY
BRIGHT

Letter Maze

Color the connecting squares that spell out
HOHOHO MERRY CHRISTMAS

C	H	H	M	R	A	R	C	H	Y
H	O	I	O	M	E	R	H	O	R
T	H	O	H	R	R	R	M	H	S
R	O	M	A	C	O	Y	I	C	T
H	O	Y	M	H	Y	C	H	R	I
Y	M	H	R	H	O	O	R	I	O
H	I	T	S	M	H	H	I	T	S
R	H	O	I	C	T	T	S	T	Y
M	H	H	I	T	S	M	A	M	Y
R	A	R	C	H	Y	A	C	A	T
I	C	T	R	H	O	S	O	S	A

Answer Keys

Pile Up the Presents

Color each path to help the
Scout Elf fill Santa's sleigh.

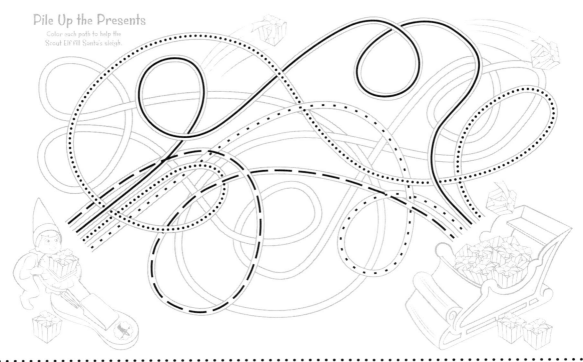

Collect Treats for the Elf Pets

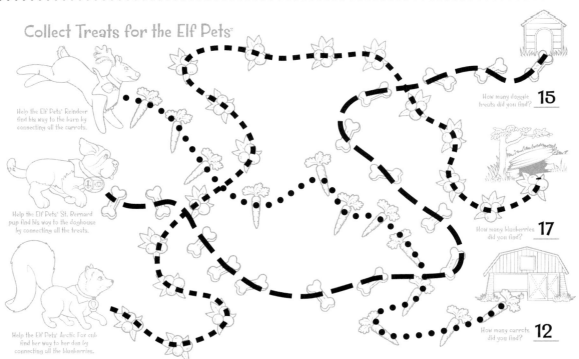

Help the Elf Pets' Reindeer
find his way to the barn by
connecting all the carrots.

Help the Elf Pets' St. Bernard
pup find his way to the doghouse
by connecting all the treats.

Help the Elf Pets' Arctic Fox cub
find her way to her den by
connecting all the blueberries.

How many doggie
treats did you find? 15

How many blueberries
did you find? 17

How many carrots
did you find? 12

Answer Keys

Find the Pikku Deer
Find and color all the Elf Pets® Reindeer.

How many Elf Pets®
Reindeer did you find?
19

Wacky Sled Race
Which path will lead you
to the finish line?

START
1 2 3

FINISH!

It's Cocoa Time!
Guide the Scout Elf to
the cup of hot cocoa.

Start Here

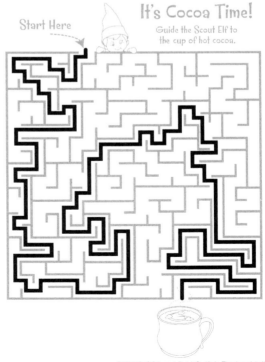

Answer Keys

❄ Snow Day Maze ❄
Help the Scout Elf and his snowman pal.

Start

Sort the Wreaths!
Help the elves find which wreath belongs to them.

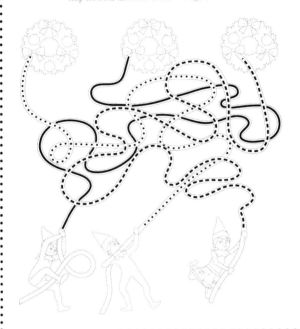

Barn Dash
Follow the carrots to find your way!

Finish

Answer Keys

Santa's Shortcut

Quick! Help Santa find the fastest way back to the North Pole.

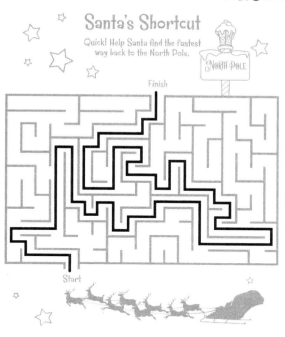

Christmas Spirit Word Search

Color the squares that spell out:
FAITH   HOPE   LOVE
Can you find the three secret words?
SCOUT ELF
SANTA CLAUS
ELF PETS' REINDEER

Christmas Star Maze

Can you find your way to the center of the Christmas Star?

String the Lights

Connect all the holiday lights by drawing only one line.

Answer Keys

This Scout Elf is Hungry!

Help him find his way
to a tasty snack.

Hidden Holiday Words

The Scout Elves have hidden eight words in this word search.
Look up, down, across and diagonally to find them.

CHRISTMAS   WREATH
PRESENTS   ELVES
TREE   SANTA
COOKIES   CANDY CANES